My name used to be Simon, but Jesus changed my name to Peter.

Put the sticker of Peter pointing to himself on this page.

1

I am a _____ _____ Jesus, my
brother and _____ _____ _____ shing boat.
We were using _____ _____ _____ to catch fish.

Put the sticker of the _____ n a net on this page.

2

Jesus called to us. "Come! Follow me," Jesus said.
My brother and I took our fishing boat to the shore,
left our boat, and followed Jesus.

Put the sticker of Jesus calling on this page.

3

Put the sticker of the large rock on this page.

One day Jesus said to me, "Simon, your faith is as strong as a rock. I will call you Peter because Peter means rock. You are Peter, and on this rock I will build my church. You will help me teach people about God!"

4

Swish, swash, splish, splash. Jesus was carrying a bowl full of water.

Jesus and the disciples had traveled a long way on roads of dirt and sand. They had dirty, gritty, smelly feet with sand between their toes!

Put the sticker of Peter with dirty feet on this page.

5

Swish, swash, splish, splash. Jesus put the bowl
of water on the floor and got down on his knees.
When Jesus tried to wash Peter's feet, Peter said,
"No, Jesus, you will not wash my feet!"

6

Put the sticker of Jesus with a bowl and towel on this page.

Jesus said to Peter, "Yes, Peter, I will wash your feet."
"But why, Jesus, are you washing my feet?" Peter asked.
"Because I love you," answered Jesus.

Put the sticker of Peter with clean feet on this page.

"Cock-a-doodle-doodle-do!" the rooster crows every morning.

Peter loved Jesus. But Jesus told Peter, "Before the rooster crows in the morning, you will tell a lie and say three times that you do not know me."

Put the sticker of Peter looking sad on this page.

8

Put the sticker of the rooster on this page.

Peter loved Jesus, but Peter was afraid because some
people were angry with Jesus.

So Peter told the angry people that he had never
known Jesus. Three times Peter said that he didn't know
Jesus!

Then Peter heard the rooster crow, "Cock-a-doodle-
doodle-do!"

Peter was sad about what he had done. But later Jesus asked Peter three questions. Three times Jesus asked, "Peter, do you love me?"

And three times Peter could say to Jesus, "Yes, Jesus, you know that I love you."

Put the sticker of Peter looking happy on this page.

10

...ter was going to the Temple to ...an who couldn't walk. The ...d. "Please," the man said to ...oney for food."

Put the sticker of a man who cannot walk on this page.

Peter said to the man, "I have no silver or gold, but what I have I gi[...]u."
The man looked at Pe[...]d Peter said to him, "In Jesus' name, sta[...]a[...]

Put the sticker of Peter hol[...]

Peter reached out and helped the man to get up and walk! The man was so excited that he jumped and danced for joy! "Praise God! Praise God!" he said.

Put the sticker of a man leaping and dancing on this page.

Peter and Cornelius were different. They lived in different cities. They ate different foods.

Put the sticker of Peter pointing with his open hand on this page.

14

Peter and Cornelius went to different churches, but they both loved God. And God loved both of them!

Put the sticker of Cornelius the soldier on this page.

God told Peter to teach Cornelius about Jesus.
God told Cornelius to teach Peter that even people
who are different love God.

Put the sticker of Peter and Cornelius on this page.